Young America

On Mustang Island, off the Gulf Coast of Texas, Jamie Link, 2, feeds the seagulls. Photo by his father, Greg Link of San Antonio, Tex.

A PICTORIAL CELEBRATION

Young America

By the Winners of the
Parade-Kodak National Photo Contest
Introduction by Walter Anderson
Continuum • New York

1990

The Continuum Publishing Company
370 Lexington Avenue
New York, NY 10017

Design by Ira Yoffe

Printed in Singapore

Library of Congress Cataloging-in-Publication Data
Young America : a pictorial celebration
by the winners of the Parade-Kodak National Photo Contest
/ introduction by Walter Anderson.
p.   cm.
ISBN 0-8264-0479-0
1. Photography of families.
2. Family—United States—Pictorial works.
I. Eastman Kodak Company.
II. Parade (New York, N.Y.)
TR681. F28Y68 1990
779′ .2′ 097307473—dc20   90-34383 CIP

"Banana George" Blair,
75, does his
one-foot-barefoot
maneuver on Lake
Florence in Winter Haven,
Fla. Photo by Matt Dunn
of Dunwoody, Ga.

This book of pictures serves many purposes. It presents a comprehensive image of American life today, depicting the people of the United States at home, at work and at play. It shows the many varied ways in which today's generation engages in that most basic of human enterprises, the pursuit of happiness.

On the purely technical side, these pictures—taken by the winners of the *Parade* magazine-Eastman Kodak Company National Photo Contest—demonstrate the sophistication and subtlety with which ordinary Americans have learned to use a camera. For the most part, the beautiful photos in this book are the work not of seasoned professionals but of avid amateurs—people who took pictures of their families, their friends, their neighbors, the world about them not for gain but for the fun of it.

That may account for the uncommon freshness and zest that characterize so many of the pictures. This is life as it is experienced, observed and enjoyed by ordinary people. Warmth, sincerity and affection shine through, along with artistry and imagination.

Above and beyond all other qualities, this book serves to redefine the word *young*. For, although the announced theme of the Parade-Kodak contest was "Young America," most of the participants chose to regard the word as meaning young in spirit, outlook, heart and hope, rather than in mere age.

Somehow, we always knew that this would be so. As the nation's most widely circulated publication, reaching more than 65 million readers every Sunday, *Parade* magazine is well aware of the enthusiasm and enterprise which Americans of all ages bring to their activities, pursuits and involvements.

This has been *Parade*'s third photo competition, and the outpouring of entries has reached an all-time high, with more than 172,000 submissions taken in all 50 states and the District of Columbia. Our distinguished judges—the photographer Eddie Adams, psychologist Dr. Joyce Brothers, model Christie Brinkley, author Alex Haley and actor Malcolm-Jamal Warner—report that they had an extremely difficult task in selecting 100 prize-winning photos from so many high-quality entries. Beyond the mere numbers, they add, they were impressed by both the tremendous variety of the submissions and the affirmation of life that seemed to bind them altogether, however different their subject matter may have been.

As you look at the pictures in this book, I believe that you too will be struck by the overall image they give of people working together productively, living together harmoniously and sharing a sense of exhilaration, affection and discovery. This picture book is an anthology of the American people today—healthy, vigorous and youthful, as we move into the last decade of the 20th century.

WALTER ANDERSON

Pals: Jessica and Mark Paden in their backyard in Birmingham, Ala. Photo by their cousin, ninth-grader Clint Blankenship of Tuscumbia, Ala.

Tea for three: Mrs. Loucinda Crews, 90, of Jacksonville, Fla., joined Miss Sara Scott, 19 months, and her friend Humphrey at a tea party. Both ladies made sure Humphrey received his fair share. Photo by Sara's mother, Debra.

Two-year-old Kristie Akamine faces a sticky situation. Photo by Roland J.C. Pang of Honolulu, Hawaii.

"To be seventy years young is sometimes far more cheerful and hopeful than to be forty years old."
— Oliver Wendell Holmes

᠄᠊

"I won't be old 'til my feet hurt, and they only hurt when I don't let 'em dance enough, so I'll keep right on dancing."
— Bill "Bojangles" Robinson

᠄᠊

"She seems to have had the ability to stand firmly on the rock of her past while living completely and unregretfully in the present."
— Madeline L'Engle

᠄᠊

"Old age has its pleasures, which, though different are not less than the pleasures of youth."
— W. Somerset Maugham

᠄᠊

*"I shall grow old, but never lose life's zest,
Because the road's last turn will be the best."*
— Henry van Dyke

13

"Eat my dust!" Leather-clad Ann Caddy, 75, slows down long enough for her daughter to snap a picture. Photo by Rosie Ann Todd of Seattle, Wash.

14

On the following page: Taking Grandpa for a ride: Doug Hollenberg, 3, and Arnold Hollenberg, 62, swap vehicles in the backyard. Photo by Doug's aunt, Judith Hollenberg of Springfield, Ill.

White-water competition: Jesse Gillis, 13 (in the bow), and Bill Hoisington, 15 (stern), run a slalom in the 1988 Open Canoe Nationals, held on the Nantahala River near Bryson City, N.C. Photo by Arvilla Brewer of Bryson City.

Tired: Patricia O'Shea, 30, and Paul Morgan, 7, enjoy one of Paul's favorite places, the main exhibit of Bigfoot 4x4 in Hazelwood, Mo. Photo by Sheila M. Chibnall-Treptow of St. Louis, Mo.

19

Rob Kelly, 15, does an "ender" in his kayak on the Youghiogheny River at School House Rock. Photo by Einar Lund of New Holland, Pa.

First-baseman Scott Gossett, 8, his game-face on, prepares to bat. Photo by Wendy L. Benes of Akron, Ohio.

Scott Evans, 3, shows off his skateboard stuff outside his home. Photo by his mother, Shari Evans of West Palm Beach, Fla.

Future champs: Hopefuls on opening day of the Little League baseball season in Kent County, Md., were (l-r) Brooke Bowman, 8, Tyrell White, 12, and Mikey Blake, 6—members of the Betterton Legion team, which went on to win the county championship. Photo by Patricia K. McGee of Chestertown, Md.

25

Randy Sauer, still spry at 74, puts plowing aside to pitch to his great-nephew Jake, 7, on the farm in Loveland, Colo. Ready to field the ball are Jake's brothers (l-r) Josh, 12, Zach, 9, and Matt, 10. The bat girl is their sister Lyndsey, 3, and the photographer is Gale Johnson Sauer.

Softball is a family game: Yvonne Cline, 67, takes her cuts while her son Warren, 39, waits in case she misses. Jeanie Cline, Warren's wife, took the photo in Lincoln, Neb.

Now batting for the "Kids": Walt Weller plays with the "Kids and Kubs" softball club in St. Petersburg, Fla. (to qualify, you must be 75 or over). Weller, 77, is a catcher. Photo by Kevin White of St. Petersburg.

And the winner is... Samia Doro, 69, crosses the finish line of the 400-meter dash at the Albuquerque Senior Olympics in New Mexico. Photo by her son, David H. Doro of Clearfield, Utah.

Kyle Winter, 5, hikes the football to female quarterback—his cousin, Natalie, also 5—during scrimmage in Buffalo Center, Iowa. Photo by Natalie's mother, Kathleen Douglass-Winter.

It's watermelon time in McCrory, Ark., with (l-r) Jon McMinn, 7, T. J. Jackson and Megan Lee, both 3, participating. Photo by Barbara Long Marlowe of McCrory.

The young desperadoes: Andrew Miller, 4 (seated), and (l-r) Jeremiah Johns, 6, Jarrett Johns, 3, James Tisdale, 3. Photo by Andrew's mother, Kim S. Miller of Gainesville, Fla.

It was good clean fun! Playmates (l-r) Matthew Long, 10, Andrew Abbott, 8, Paige Abbott, 4, and Tyson Abbott, 6. Photo by Richard N. Abbott Jr. of Boone, N.C.

Before the jamboree: Bassist Keith King gets plenty of assistance from family and friends at the Pioneer Campground Bluegrass Festival in Lake Village, Ind. L-r: Kari King, 2, Henry Maul, 8, Jesse King, 4, Keith King, 36, Christy Sandage, 4, Adam King, 8. Photo by Edie Hamernik of Crown Point, Ind.

Back to back are Tim Guyette, 7, and Curtis Backus, 10, in Glens Falls, N.Y. Photo by Robert Mosher of Sandusky, Ohio.

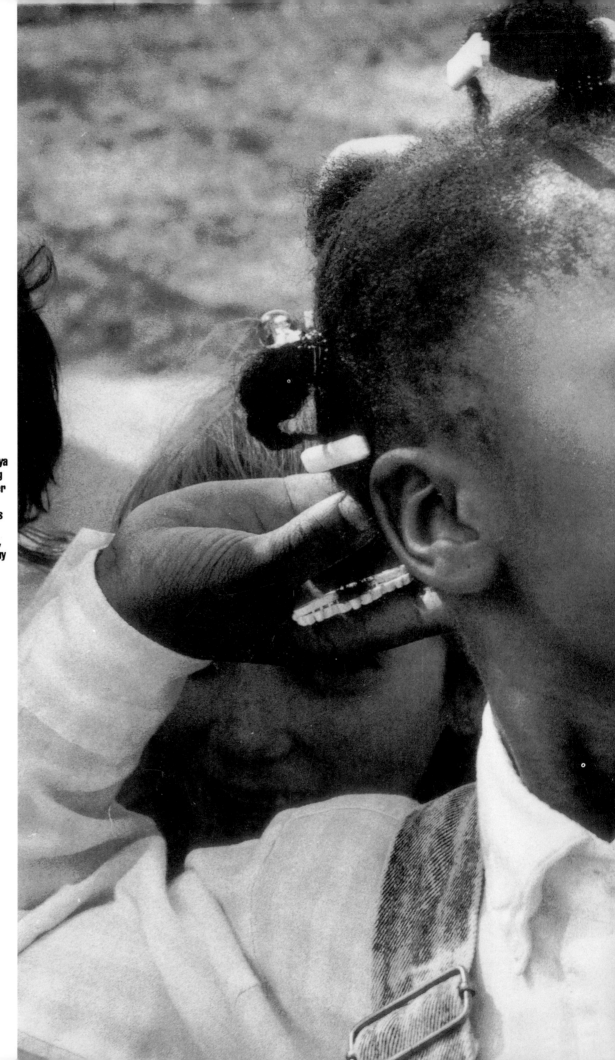

"Aren't I pretty?" Nekeya Dancy, 7, poses during recess at Martin Luther King Jr. School in Cambridge, Mass., as Lisa Cooper, 8, and Monique Davidson, 9, enjoy the show. Photo by Margot Ouellet of Watertown, Mass.

Marisa Bacoats, 7, gets a surprise kiss from her brother Gerald, 4, at her first Holy Communion, in Blessed Trinity Catholic Church, St. Petersburg, Fla. Photo by their mother, Laura Bacoats of Tierra Verde, Fla.

"Camille [l] and Christopher, both about 18 months, are good friends. It was a surprise to me—and to Christopher—when Camille thought a little kiss would be nice," says the photographer, Gary L. Puttuck of Salt Lake City, Utah.

Look into my eyes: Amanda Braden, 1 year old, and her brother Drew, 3, communicate soulfully. Photo by Cheril G. De Koekkoek of Bellflower, Calif.

**Growing up: Emily Smith, 12, and Jason Bell, 15, of Fort Washington, Pa.
Photo by Staff Sgt. Jerry Baker, U.S. Air Force, of League City, Tex.**

Isn't it romantic? This photo of "Spike" and Amy Davis was taken at LaBagh Woods in Chicago for their wedding invitation. Photo by Terrence Wheeler of Chicago.

Enjoying an ice cream soda together are Ann and John Barton, 75 and 76 respectively. They were on a visit from their Pennsylvania home to Costa Mesa, Calif., where their granddaughter, Rebecca Visca of Huntington Beach, Calif., took this picture.

Dressed for dinner: Jonathan Pelts, 5 months old, prepares to partake. (Jonathan's fancy tux is actually a sleeping outfit, complete with tails, a gift from his Aunt Mary Ann.) Photo by his dad, Wayne Pelts of Bluefield, W. Va.

Double-header: Dan Evans and his grandson, Nathan, share a view of Corey Lake, Mich. Photo by Christopher Evans of Chesterton, Ind.

On previous page: Stephen Tanaka, 6, on Lake Winnott in Hawthorne, Fla. "Stephen rows himself out on the lake and fishes all the time. I just captured his ritual at sunset," says the photographer, Cheryl S. M. Corindia of Marietta, Ga.

Looking for signs of life in a creek behind her house in Dry Creek Valley, Calif., is 2-year-old Jessica Schwartz. Photo is by her mother, Kelly Schwartz.

Danny Koenig, 16, plays solo soccer under a tree radiant with
sunbeams in Stockton, Calif. Photo by Scott Sady of Lodi, Calif.

Two-year-old Kristina Richards was photographed by her father, Gareth L. Richards of Moreno Valley, Calif. Driving along a freeway, he saw these flower fields, set Kristina among them and snapped the shutter.

On her first visit to a beach, Sara Ann Moline, 13 months, discovers an interesting new creature. Photo by her father, Gregory Thomas Moline of Lake Zurich, Ill.

First, you crawl: Nine-month-old Amanda Kathryn Hoey covers some territory on the beach at Kiawah Island, S.C. Photo by Anne McConnell of Gortin, Ireland, a student visitor to the U.S.

"Has anyone down here seen my bathing suit?" asks Morgan McCauley, 6 months old, as he skinny-dips in the family pool. Photo by his father, William P. McCauley of Ocean Ridge, Fla.

Fully equipped for diving is Kelley Emil Richards, 5, photographed by his uncle, Robert L. Ensminger, at the family pool in Carmichael, Calif.

Water baby: Aidan Bryant, 2, of Phoenix, Ariz., loves winging it in the pool. Aidy's grandmother, Wylene Vinall of Tucson, took this photo.

63

Swimming with friend is
10-month-old Kelsey
Schmidt of Ballston Spa,
N.Y. Photo by Teresa
Levine of Bellingham,
Mass.

The Austrian Maidens, students at the Lake Mills School of Dance, perform in a special program at the L.D. Fargo Public Library in Lake Mills, Wis. Naomi Fenske faces the camera. Photo by Robert R. Heussner of Lake Mills.

" The power to animate all of life's seasons is a power that resides within us. "
— Gail Sheehy

❧

" When nothing is sure, everything is possible. "
— Margaret Drabble

❧

" Anyone who keeps the ability to see beauty never grows old. "
— Franz Kafka

❧

" It is the mind that makes the body. "
— Sojourner Truth

❧

" Nothing great was ever achieved without enthusiasm. "
— Ralph Waldo Emerson

Little Larisa-Iize Lazdins
starts practicing for the
Winter Olympics at the
ice rink at Countryside
Mall in Clearwater, Fla.
Photo by Pete C. Lucchini
of New Port Richey, Fla.

Thirteen feet are in over their heads, celebrating the 10th birthday of Erin Prevatt last May 10 in Orlando, Fla. Photo by Erin's aunt, Barbara A. Kelly of Long Beach, Calif., who bought the brightly colored socks as party favors.

What a paradise it seems! July 4th, the Anclote River, Fla.: Rhett Mullinax (l), Jeremy Mullinax (airborne), Vanya Mullinax, Gordon Mullinax (back to camera). Photo by Jane Blake of Seminole, Fla.

And away we go! Three generations take a plunge at Lake Mystic in Bristol, Fla. L-r: Lynn Long, 32, Allan Pratt, 58 and Shanna Reznik, 8. Photo by Liz Pendergrass of Indian Rocks Beach, Fla.

Is it Superman? Well, yes and no. Michael Dorociak of Sarasota, Fla., was photographed by his wife, Shawn G. Dorociak, at Hollywood Beach, Fla., during an afternoon off from his dental residency.

Zest! Nita Reeves, 61, of Florence, Miss., has won the National Water Ski Championship for her age group (55 plus) for the last three years. Photo by her husband, Billy.

Sail away: Larry Yount, 74, and his dog spend a fine summer day on Lake Sammamish in Redmond, Wash. Photo by Peggy Yount.

"Your eyes...the color of a clear blue lake": Christina Ann Clark, 7, swimming in Canada Lake, N.Y.
Photo by her grandfather, Edward R. Younglove of Johnstown, N.Y.

Summer swirl: Jill Henke, 9, cools off at the Athletic Center pool in The Woodlands, Tex. Photo by her mother, Joan Henke.

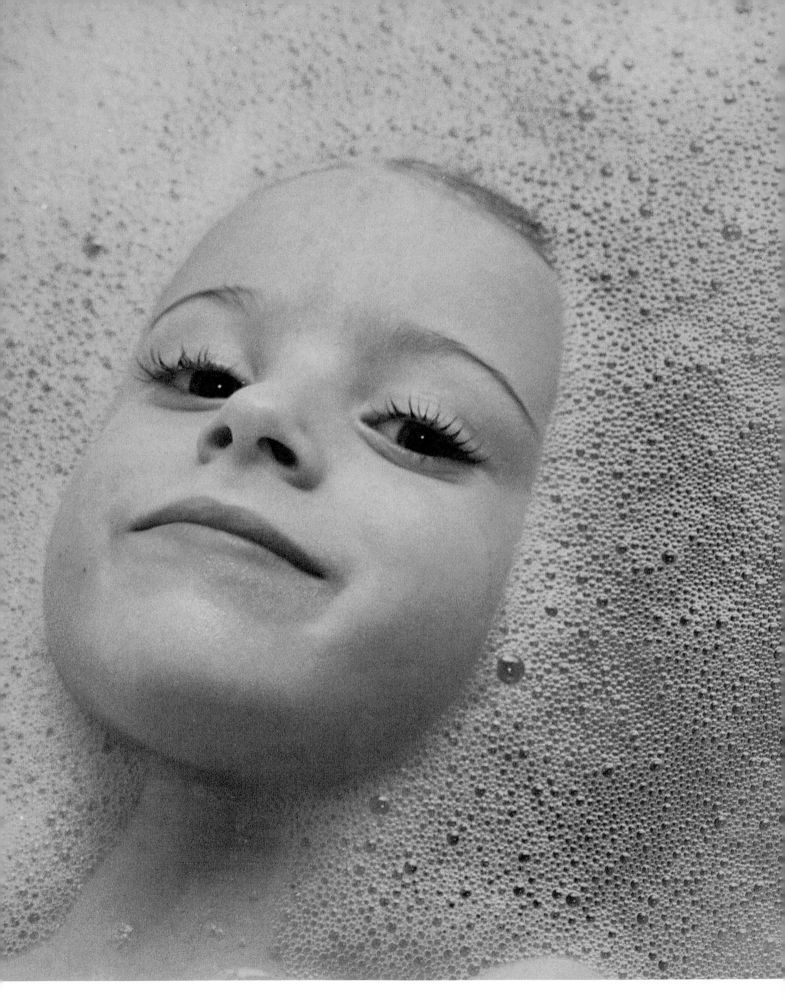

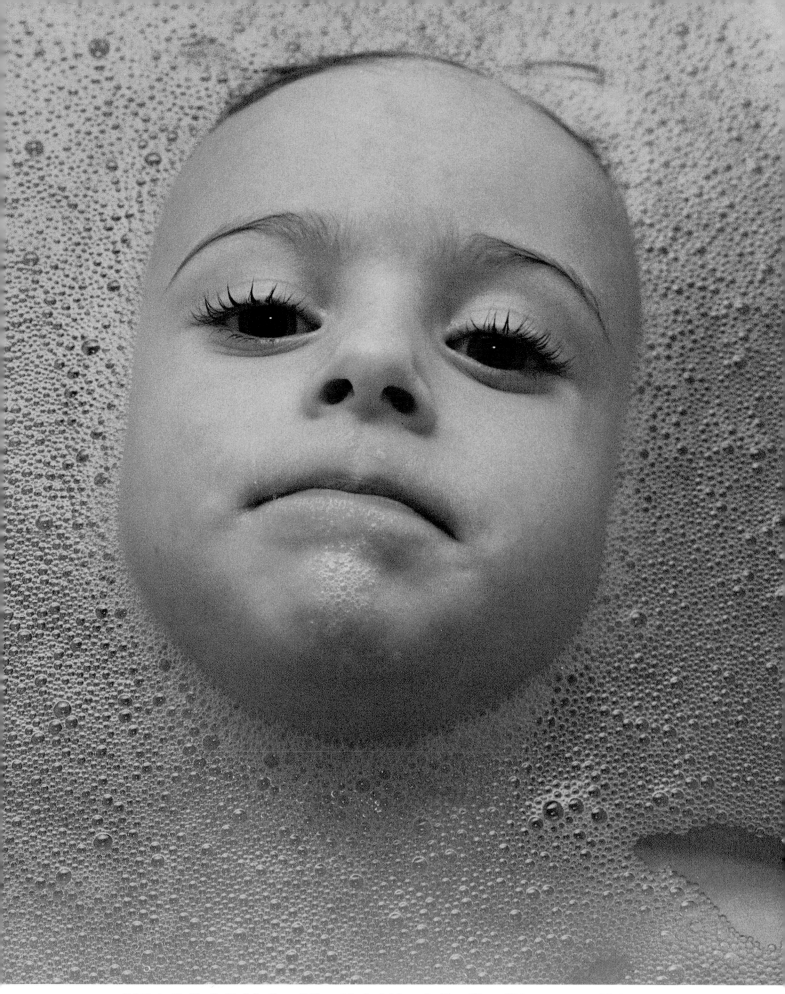

Bubble double: Identical twin brothers, Robby and Jordan Lefebvre, 4, of Grand Haven, Mich., were so peaceful at bath time one day that when their dad, Raymond, peeked in to check, he had to photograph them.

We'll grow up together: Gail Tramontano of Hackettstown, N.J., took this photo of her son, Matthew, 2, with his pet, Madame Haiku, 1, at Grandma's house in West Point Island, N.J.

Julianna Barile and her dog, Reggie, near Long Lake in New York State's Adirondack mountains. Julianna was "almost 2," says her aunt, Susan Ann Butler of Cambridge, Mass., who took the picture.

Maddie the trusty Weimaraner makes sure that Kevin Page, 10 months, finishes his milk. Photo by Elizabeth J. Page of Braintree, Mass.

Stuck. Kelsey Resa, 9 months, and the family dog, T.J., probably wish they were out exploring. Photo by Kelsey's mom, Angela B. Resa of Leonard, Mo.

Little bull-rider Dylan Pospisil, 10 months, atop "Billy," a Brahman bull, in Austin, Tex. Photo by his mother, Mary Lou Pospisil of Austin.

Whoa! At the semi-annual ropin', brandin' and ridin' event at his grandparents' ranch in Langell Valley near Bonanza, Ore., Doug Howland, 8, hops on, his dad holds onto his belt loop, the rope is loosened...and up jumps the calf! Photo by Donna Springer Howland of Klamath Falls, Ore.

Little boy, big job: Ryan Kramer, 5, has a treat for purebred Belgian draft horses on Rock Falls Farm in Harbor Beach, Mich. Photo by Todd Bingham of Ruth, Mich.

Larry Rinderknecht of Marion, Iowa, may have been a mere 18 months old when his dad, Duane, snapped this photo in the summer of '71, but the duck let the toddler know he'd made one quack too many.

Linnea Wellnau, 7, competes in the greased-pig contest at Erie County Junior Fair in Sandusky, Ohio. She won! Photo by Robin Layton of Glen Allen, Va.

Close encounter: Rosann Dovak, 4, meets a
bee in her backyard. Photo by her mother,
Pamela Dovak of Islip Terrace, N.Y.

That's a friendly frog
4-year-old Jessica Lynn
Robertson is holding in
her front yard in
Mansfield, Ohio. Her
father, Jeff Robertson,
took the picture.

Carson Wann (l) and his friend Brian George, both 3, get a good look at a blimp at the Wiley Post Airport in Oklahoma City, Okla. Photo by Kitty Dillon of Memphis, Tenn.

This is the life! Travis McMurray, 2, soaks up the atmosphere in his backyard while his mother, Cynthia Dawn McMurray of Metairie, La., snaps the picture.

M…I…SEE: Elizabeth Sweitzer, 2, may not know about the Mickey Mouse Club yet, but she has a clear-eyed view of the world. Her mom, Sheri L. Sweitzer, took this photo at their home in Washington, D.C.

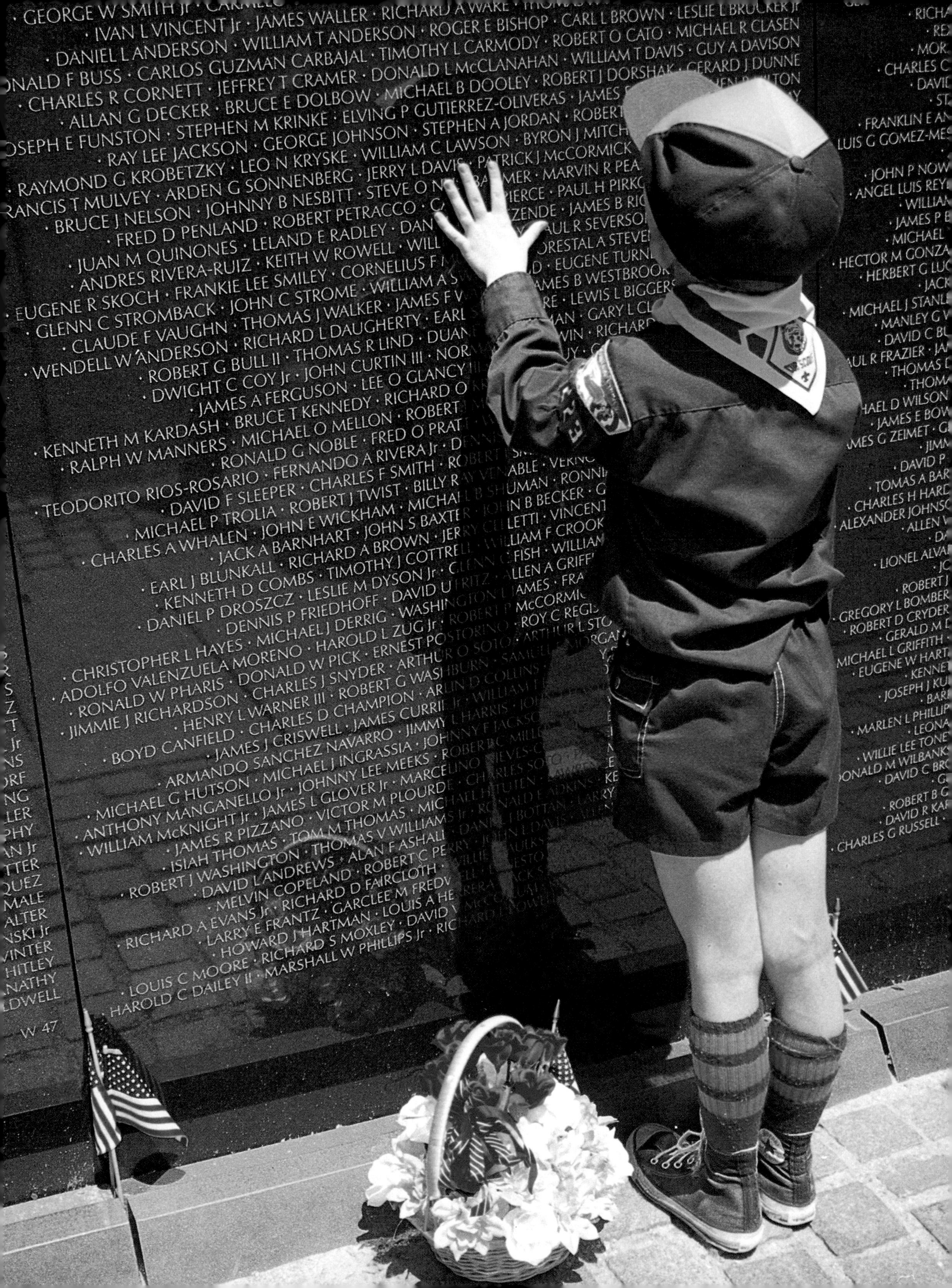

For Miles Maassen, 10 months, happiness is an old wheelbarrow on a late spring
afternoon. Photo by his mother, Karen Maassen of Goleta, Calif.

This is how: Baker Giduz, 2, shows everyone how his grandfather taught him to make a funny face. Photo by Bill Giduz of Davidson, N.C.

Inclined to have fun: Roberta Bain, 73, zips down the sand hills of Monahans State Park in Texas. Photo by her son, William Bain of Falls Church, Va.

"Oh, Daddy, you sure look pretty now!" Robb Furstenfeld checks out his new coiffure, courtesy of daughter Ashley, 3. Photo by her mom, Pamela D. Furstenfeld of Pinehurst, Tex.

Caught! One-year-old Justin Smith was playing with photographer Tony Deifell's flash unit one dark night in a field outside Mocksville, N.C. Suddenly—pop!—everything lit up. Justin's face lit up even more, and Tony—who's from Clearwater, Fla.—alertly pointed the camera.

Barely awake: Chessa Rose Anderson's first Christmas.
Photo by Kelly DeHaven of Madison, Wis.

Photographer Chris Wimpey of San Diego, Calif., takes monthly pictures to record his son Zachary's growth. In this one, Zachary, 8 months old, surprises his mother, Brenda Bodney.

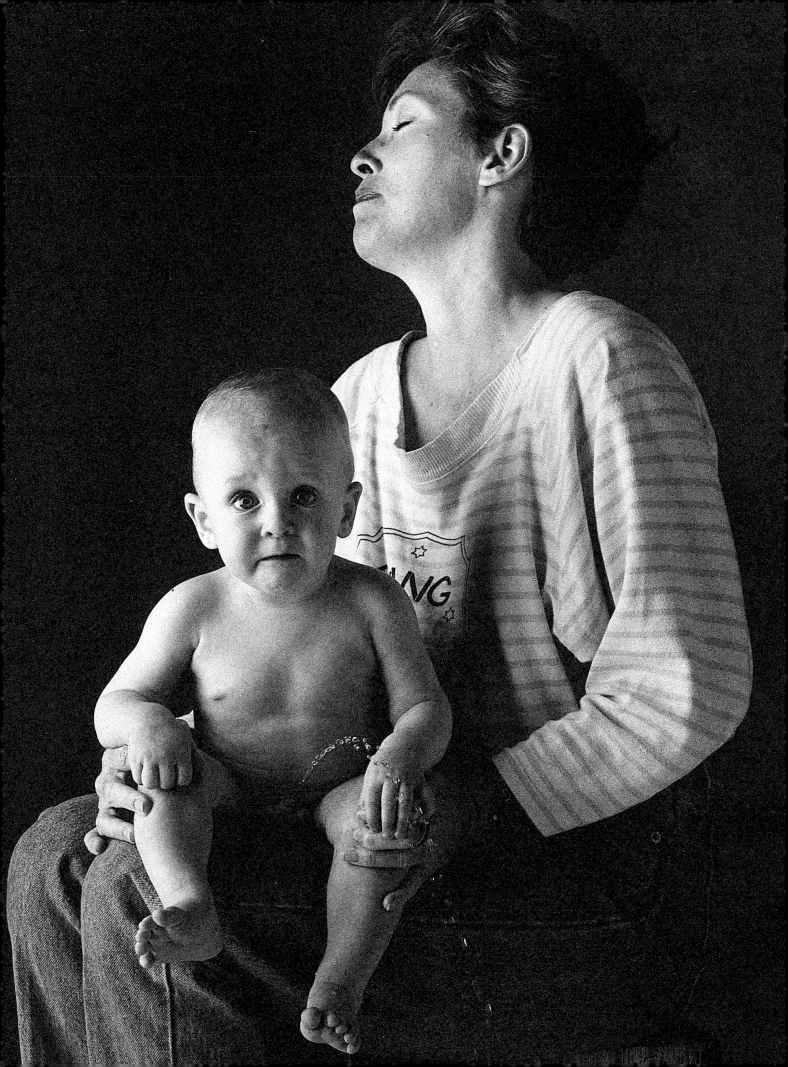

Baby dolls: Decked out in curls and white lace,
Caroline Guman, 3, and her doll pose prettily.
Photo by Angela Storey of Morehead City, N.C.

Strawberry fields:
Elizabeth Bartholomew, 11
months, takes part in the
pickings at Wilhelm's
Farm in Wilsonville, Ore.
Photo by her mother,
Susan of Portland, Ore.

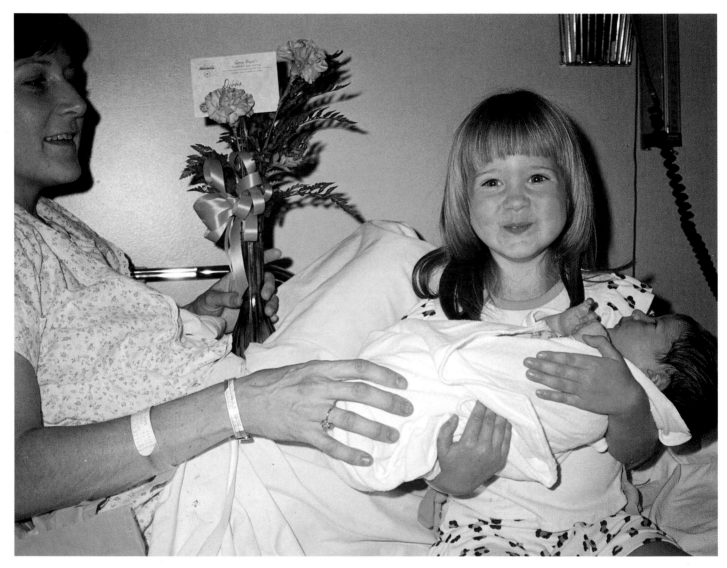

Shanna Perz, 4, gives her mother, Debbie, a hand with new little sister, Jessica—born just 12 hours earlier. Photo by the proud papa, Joseph T. Perz of Clearwater, Fla.

Father's first visit with the twins: Alan Dillon of Manassas, Va., holds 3-day-old twins Kasey and Krystin in Potomac Hospital. Photo by their mother, Brenda.

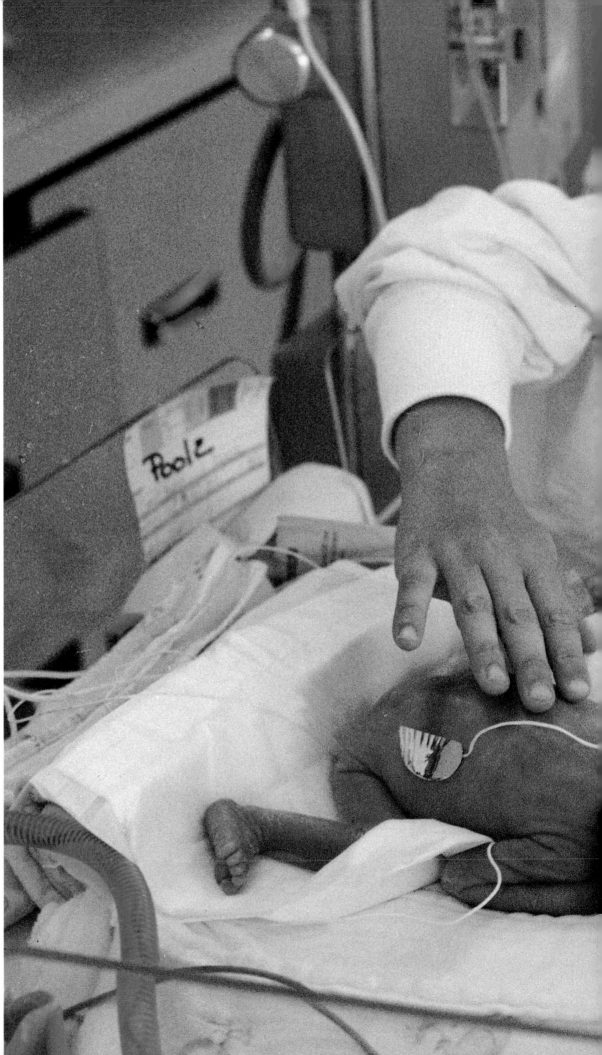

Welcome to the family: Melissa Poole, 8, greets her new brother, Daniel, for the first time at the ICU nursery of The Woman's Hospital of Texas. Photo by their father, Terry Poole of Hockley, Tex.

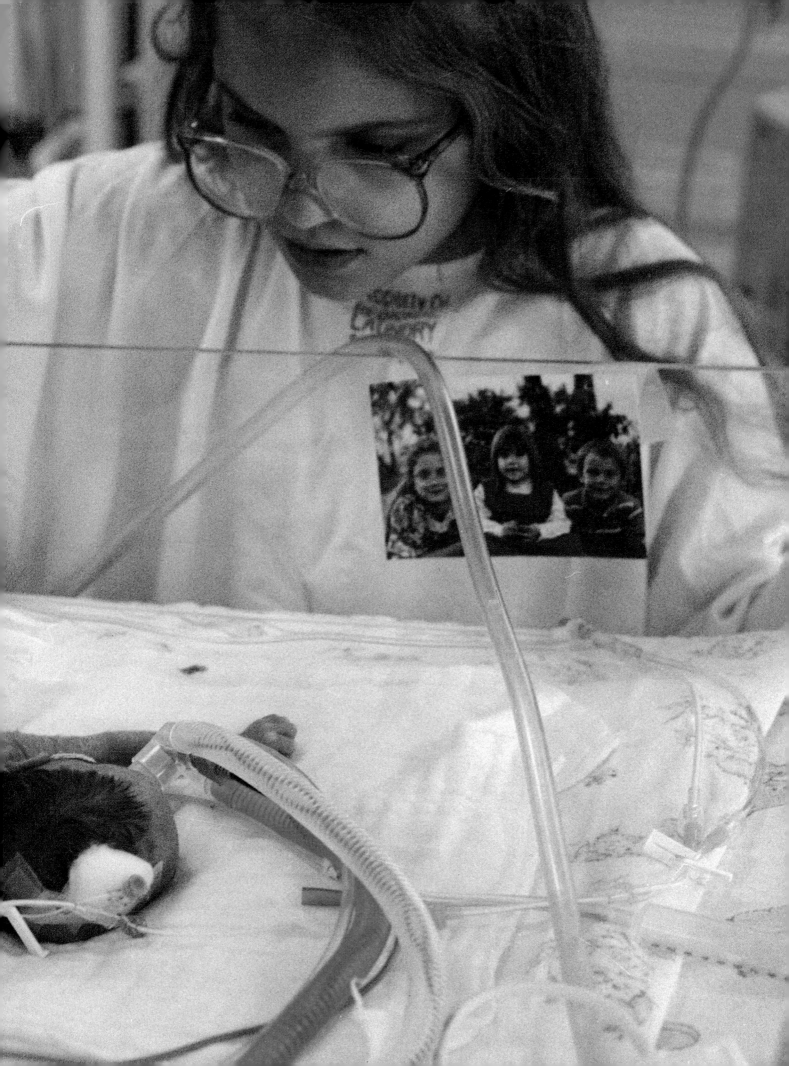

Taking her ease on a beat-up hammock is 5-year-old Jacque Rae
of Dallas, Tex. Photo by Don Tremain of Dallas.

Clay Quinby, 6, who is still learning how to blow bubbles, just saw his father pop a big one. Photo by Clay's mother, Dianne Quinby of High Point, N.C.

A foot at a time: Merynn Ito, 3, finds a way to cool off on a warm summer day at Nuuanu Reservoir in Honolulu, Hawaii. Photo by Dean Y. Ohtani of Honolulu.

"Me, Tarzan. You, Jane": Mighty mite Mathew Pittelli, 5, flexes his biceps for Lisa Giampoala, also 5, but she seems unimpressed. Photo by Sal Trombino of Little Falls, N.J.

Liberty victorious: Ashley Whelan, 1, lifts her lamp upon being named a winner in the patriotic-costume competition last July 4 at the Lynnhurst School in Saugus, Mass. Photo by M.K. Rynne of Nahant, Mass.

Two grandmothers: Mildred Douglas (l), 82, and Amanda Wright, 85, on the beach at St. Petersburg, Fla. Photo by their grandson-in law, David Michael Martin of Germantown, Md.

California girl: For Ashley Alderson, 3, on a May afternoon at San Clemente Beach, Calif., life's just super. Photo by Patricia Gasser of Laguna Hills, Calif.

Pacifying father: Seven-month-old Marshall has a present for Dad, Daniel Clayton, at Atlantic Beach, Fla. Photo by Mom, Celia Clayton of Jacksonville.

Grandfather and child: T. R. Moncure, 75, and Catherine Boysen, 1, give each other the once-over. Photo by Janet Moncure of Mechanicsville, Va.

Family portrait: Eight-month-old Brandon Joseph Smith and his great-grandmother, May Belle Mitchell, 81—each thinks the other looks funny. Photo by David Smith, Brandon's father and May Belle's grandson, of Auburn, Ala.

Mattie Allison, 15 months, with her Groucho-lookalike grandparents, Harriet and Norman Allison, both 75, of Bloomfield Hills, Mich. Photo by Kaye Allison of Fairfax, Va.

Bridging the age barrier: Allan Charles Orr of Youngstown, Ohio (who also took the photo), painted the portrait of his son, Zachary, 7, while Zachary rendered his grandfather, Willis Orr, in oils and pastels.

A family reunion: Monica Maner, 7, with her great-grandmother, Florence Bingler, 90, on the front porch in Charlottesville, Va. Photo by Monica's mother, Valorie Maner of Knoxville, Tenn.

Boy with boots: Andrew Cahoon, 5, watches as his father competes in the draught horse weight-pulling at the Virginia State Fair. Photo by P. Kevin Morley of Richmond.

66 Lambs skip and bound, kittens and puppies seem wild with the joy of life; and little children naturally run, leap, dance and shout in the exuberance of that capacity for happiness which the young human heart feels as instinctively as the flower buds open to the sun. 99
— Emma Hart Willard

❧

66 Oh for one hour of youthful joy! 99
— Oliver Wendell Holmes

❧

66 Youth…through it alone shall salvation come. 99
— Helen Keller

❧

66 Childhood smells of perfume and brownies. 99
— David Leavitt
Family Dancing

❧

66 A baby is God's opinion that the world should go on. 99
— Carl Sandburg
Remembrance Rock

Warming the bench at Ginn Field in Winchester, Mass., are Andrew Christopher, 4, and three older teammates. Photo by Sharon M. Sullivan of Cambridge, Mass.

Sky-high: John Kenyon, 31, and David Kenyon, 28, are more than happy as they reach the summit of Mount Hunger in the Worcester Range of Vermont. Photo by Mary Anne Murphy of South Braintree, Mass.

EDDIE ADAMS

Everybody thinks it's cameras that take pictures, but actually people do. That may seem obvious but it's a simple truth that I think too often gets overlooked and one that cannot be repeated often enough. For example, you can know everything there is to know about photography, be a genius technically, but your picture still can come out sterile. That's why I like to say the best pictures are taken from the heart. This is especially true today when the camera is so advanced that the average person taking a picture doesn't have to fool with distance, light and so on, and can just concentrate on taking the shot, from the heart and from the hip. It comes down to having that special sense, the right awareness for the right time, the right moment—and keeping your camera handy. Always. Always be ready. This book is about the young, at any age, I think it shows how the best photographs have fresh, almost innocent childlike elements: wonder, surprise, sensitivity and feeling. Every photographer often wishes he had the eyes of a child, so he can see things new, see a world where nothing—not one thing—is boring, a world where he's always discovering something. Another kind of something happens to us as we grow up so that our thoughts, our ideas, our imaginations, even, sometimes regrettably, our hearts harden and we lose our capacity for knowing the freshness of things, for recognizing richness lying free before us.

There are many wonderful pictures in this book. In fact, I like them all. That's why I voted for them. All exemplify in one way or another the theme of youthful spirit and of photographers who shoot from the heart.

I have to say that one of my favorites—the one of the little boy sitting in his mother's lap while nature takes its course and his mother looks away in good-humored despair—really succeeds because of the element of surprise. It's sound technically, but what really causes it to succeed is the fact that it's so warm, and so funny. We need more humor in photography and in the world. We tend to take everything too seriously. I love a picture like this. It brings a smile.

CHRISTIE BRINKLEY

When I was asked to be a judge for the "Young America" Photo Contest, I was delighted. Photography has been an integral part of my life for many years. At 18, I went to Paris and began my modeling career. With a lot of luck and some hard work, I made a success of it. I've had the pleasure of working with some of the best photographers in the world.

If being in front of the camera is my career, being behind it is my passion. I take pictures of everything from prize fights to my beautiful daughter. Shooting photos is even more fun than posing for them. Judging photos is another story. The quality and range of the photos the other judges and I were asked to view were quite amazing, which made the selection difficult at times, but always interesting. The spirit of youthfulness has been captured in so many ways. Whether young in years or young at heart, young Americans abound and their images have been caught in the fine winning photos in this book.

DR. JOYCE BROTHERS

Being part of young America is not a matter of chronological age, it's a matter of attitude.

Simply, it's being childlike—not childish—and seeing things with wonder: clearly, and with delight; as they are, and not as we distort them, through filters of personal prejudice and preconceived notions. Picasso once wrote that he had to learn to paint as an adult before he could paint as a child. He knew that it is this childlike attitude which makes us age creatively, which makes young people learn effectively, which makes living an adventure.

Traditionally, Americans have lived in the here and now and in the future. But perhaps for the first time, as a nation, Americans are looking back as well. We remain a young America but cherish and are aware of our past—our heritage. Once concerned with knocking down old buildings to build new ones, we are preserving old edifices, finally hearing the wisdom of our elders and acknowledging the truth in the cliché that you can't keep reinventing the wheel.

We've developed a past worth treasuring, worth building upon in the present to make our country's future brighter. In these pictures, we see a continuum and some of them delight us and evoke our laughter—they urge us to laugh at ourselves and not to take ourselves too seriously, one of the barometers of mental health for our country. There are several such barometers for personal and national mental health: being sensitive to and enjoying beauty; relating to people and caring about them; having a sense of humor about ourselves and the world and its troubles. All of these pictures show an exuberance and an emotional balance.

In many of these pictures (tea party, p.5. especially), we could switch generations (the old woman and the infant girl reflect one another, reflect simultaneously for us all where we've been, where we're going and the fun we can expect along the way). The child within us all stays with us through the years. Whether we're 19 months or 90 years old, we can pretend to be bigger than life at a tea party with tiny cups and at 7 or 77, our hearts and souls soar at the crack of ball against bat as we give our all and run for home.

ALEX HALEY

"**Y**oung America!" Just saying the words allows one to conjure up so many rich images.

America…a young, innovative country full of so many varied, vital people, all of us different but all of us American. And just as there are so many different kinds of people that make up this country—the true melting pot—there are myriad ways of being young. It is a state of mind, a state of being, a state of soul much more than a state of years. Chronological age has very little to do with being young, and this truth was reflected in the thousands of pictures entered into the "Young America" photo contest.

Happiness, in its many manifestations, beams from all faces. The feeling of well-being that comes from happiness is indeed a precious commodity, and these photographs give off that feeling in abundance. The viewer can take inspiration from these pictures and feel better just by seeing them. That communication is what makes all of these photos terrific successes.

It is my good fortune to have been asked to be a judge for this national contest.

The breadth and quality of the photographs submitted was astonishing. The inquisitiveness of babies, the unbridled energy of children, the steady, fun-loving adults, the twinkling vitality of the elderly—all are here in the winning photographs on these pages. Look at them closely. You will see and feel "Young America" in all its many forms, all its many guises, all its many ages.

MALCOLM JAMAL WARNER

When I was asked to be a judge for Parade's Young America Photo Contest, I expected to look at a lot of pictures of babies, toddlers and teenagers. However, I was surprised and inspired by the thousands of submissions showing people of all ages doing what they do best—enjoying life! All of these winning photographs show how we continually search for and find ways to make ourselves happy.

As an actor and filmmaker, I value the power of a camera. What other object can capture a moment in time that can be shared with others and treasured forever?

One of the best things about working on the Cosby show is the steady influx of youth it provides. Whether we're doing an episode about a three-year-old's birthday or a family tribute to our grandparents' anniversary, where we perform old songs with a newer, upbeat arrangement, the theme of the show remains the same—to keep things lively, fresh and young.

I like the 100 pictures that I chose because they reflect my idea of Young America as a state of mind, not an age. And I think that after looking at these pictures you will come away with a sense of warmth, humor and appreciation for the human spirit.